# WILDLIFE
## PORTRAITS IN WOOD

**30 Patterns to Capture the Beauty of Nature**

Charles Dearing

T0347051

FOX CHAPEL
PUBLISHING

**CHARLES DEARING** currently resides in Round Rock, Texas. His artistic talents became evident at an early age, but he didn't discover the joys of scrolling until later in life. For Charles, scrolling became an addiction. He started creating his own designs when he couldn't find commercial patterns to meet his needs. He continues to strive for success, mainly driven by the love he has for his beautiful daughter, Kacey. Visit Charles' website at *www.BullRunArt.com*.

## Dedication

This book is dedicated to my precious daughter Kacey, my parents, and my siblings, who are my biggest fans.

I want to thank Fox Chapel Publishing for making this book possible and Steve at Woodstock in Liberty Hill, Texas, for helping me get exposure for my work. I also want to thank Tom Mullane, Darryn Armstrong, Gary Corey, Pat Lupori, Gary Earl, Rick Hutcheson, Brian Gerving, and Randall Reed for their support and encouragement, and all the scrollers who have ordered patterns from me along the way.

—Charles Dearing

Alan Giagnocavo – *President*
Shannon Flowers – *Editor*
Troy Thorne – *Creative Director*
Jon Deck – *Layout*

© 2007 by Fox Chapel Publishing Company, Inc.

*Wildlife Portraits in Wood* is an original work, first published in 2007 by Fox Chapel Publishing Company, Inc. Readers may make copies of these patterns for personal use. The patterns themselves, however, are not to be duplicated for resale or distribution under any circumstances. Any such copying is a violation of copyright law.

ISBN 978-1-56523-338-6

Dearing, Charles, 1970-

    Wildlife portraits in wood: 30 patterns to capture the beauty of nature / Charles Dearing. -- East Petersburg, PA : Fox Chapel Publishing, c2007.

        p. ; cm.
        ISBN: 978-1-56523-338-6
        1. Wood-carving--Technique. 2. Wood-carving--Patterns.
    3. Wildlifewood-carving--Patterns. 4. Jig saws. I. Title.

TT199.7 .D43 2007
736/.4--dc22                   0712

To learn more about other great books from Fox Chapel Publishing, or to find a retailer near you, call toll-free 1-800-457-9112 or visit us at *www.FoxChapelPublishing.com*.

Printed in Singapore
Second printing

**Note to Authors:** We are always looking for talented authors to write new books. Please send a brief letter describing your idea to Acquisition Editor, 1970 Broad Street, East Petersburg, PA 17520.

# CONTENTS

It's easy to design your own portrait-style scroll saw pattern. To get started, all you need is a good source image. The image should be in focus and have good contrast between the light and dark areas. You can then create a derivative work based on that image that is suitable for cutting on the scroll saw. There are several different methods for converting the image into a scroll saw pattern, but I've found tracing the image and drafting a hard copy gives me the most artistic freedom. In this section, we'll begin by choosing a photo to use for a pattern. Once you have selected an image, you can follow the demonstration to create your own pattern. Equally important are the methods you use to cut and display your work, and I've included a few tips from my own experience in those areas as well.

## CHOOSING A GOOD IMAGE

The most important step when creating a pattern is to make certain you are not violating a copyright. Portrait-style patterns are usually created from a photograph or painting. Creating a scroll saw pattern from an existing image is essentially creating a derivative work based on the original image. If you did not take the photo yourself, you need to make sure you have permission to make a pattern from it. The easiest way to ensure you are not in violation of a copyright is to use a public domain photo. Images in the public domain have either been made available to the general public by the original artist or the copyright has expired. A web search for public domain images will produce a number of sources.

If you do plan to use a copyrighted image, you must get written permission from the original artist. This may be easier than you think. Many artists simply want credit for their creation. Others will ask for payment for a derivative work to be made from the image. When contacting the artist, show them samples of your work. If you are going to make a gift for a friend or family member, tell them that. If you are designing patterns to sell the finished project at craft shows, or intend to sell the actual patterns, it's important to communicate your intentions. Also make it clear that you will be providing credit to them as the source for the original image.

In addition to making sure you can legally use the image, you need to make sure the image is suitable for pattern making. Start with the largest photo you can find. Many images you find on the Internet have been reduced in size so the web pages load faster. When you enlarge these images to print them out, they get blurry, and you have to guess about some details. If you are using the images as a reference, this is fine, but I suggest you use the biggest images you can find for your first few patterns. No matter how big you make the pattern, you can reduce the size when you reproduce it for cutting (on a photocopier or when you print it from a computer). Keep in mind that what looks

easy to cut at 11" x 17" may be difficult to cut at 8½" x 11".

I'll often bring the photo into an image manipulation program, such as Photoshop or Paint Shop Pro, and crop out the section of the image I want to use. This allows you to concentrate on the portion you intend to convert to a pattern and saves printer ink. I also use a program like this to scan in my completed pattern and troubleshoot the design.

When you enlarge the original photo, you'll notice that you lose resolution and the image becomes pixilated. On the enlargements at right, the top photo is suitable for tracing, while the bottom one makes it difficult to determine where the pattern lines should be drawn.

## Functional Patterns

When I initially draw my pattern, I leave the positive areas, or areas I want to remain solid wood, white. The negative spaces, or waste areas to be removed, are shaded. In order for the pattern to be functional, the white areas must be connected, and the shaded areas must be large enough to be cut out.

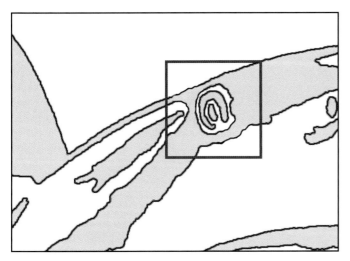

The eye is often a troublesome area. Notice that the white areas do not connect, producing a "floater" which will fall out when cut.

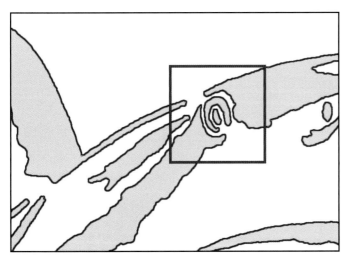

By connecting the white or wood areas, you eliminate the floater and create a functional pattern.

When many artists first begin designing patterns, they run into the problem of "floaters." Floaters are areas of wood that are meant to be in the final design, but are not connected to anything. All of the white areas have to be connected to other white areas. If they aren't, you'll have a picture that will fall apart when you cut it. The areas that connect the white sections together are called "bridges." Some artists intentionally leave floaters to convey their design, but these areas must be glued separately to the backing board.

There is no law saying that you have to trace exactly what you see. If there are a lot of shadows, you can break them up by tracing them in sections. Only you know how much shadow or negative space you want to cut out. Portrait-style cutting, as with most scroll saw projects, deals only in black and white. There is wood present, or there is negative space. There is no in-between.

Finally, the pattern must "hold water." This is where the "fill" function on your software program comes in handy. After you have the pattern drafted, scan it into your software and use the fill function to shade the negative spaces. If your shading spills out into areas that are meant to remain white, you may be missing a line. The fill function also helps to highlight any floaters that you may not have previously noticed. All negative space areas, or areas of wood to be removed, should be a closed circuit. Look at a simple shape, such as a circle. It has no beginning and no end—it's a closed circuit. It'll hold water; therefore, it can be cut out.

## Pattern Detail

As a pattern designer, you will need to make certain judgement calls and take some liberties with your original image. For example, if you want to create a pattern of an individual wearing a hat where the shadow is falling over their eyes, you could create that shadow as negative space, but you would lose most of the details of the image. Instead, you could choose to ignore most of that shadow, and bring out the details of the face. You don't need to represent every shadow as negative space in the pattern.

The more detail you include in your pattern, the more difficult the project will be to cut. Sometimes you can get carried away with trying to include too much detail in your pattern, and you actually end up detracting from the finished piece. If it is difficult to discern what the main image is on the pattern, the finished project will be difficult to interpret as well. Sometimes suggestion of detail can be just as effective as existing detail.

## Software Sources

Paint Shop Pro: *www.corel.com*

Photoshop: *www.adobe.com*

Gimp: *www.gimp.org*

Paint: *www.microsoft.com* (automatically installed with most versions of Windows)

## MAKING A PATTERN

Many would-be pattern designers struggle with technology to create their designs. There are a variety of software programs on the market that enable artists to convert images to patterns. Some are more user-friendly than others. However, the downfall of many of these programs is that you don't have the option of choosing which details to include. The program will convert the entire photograph. I find using these types of programs to break a photograph down into layers and change the lines into vector-based graphics is more trouble than it's worth. I prefer to keep it simple and use paper and pen. This method also allows me more freedom to choose which elements of the photograph to use in my pattern.

▲ **Step 1: Choose the image.** Find a picture you like, enlarge it to the size you want, and print it out on regular paper. Remember to respect the copyrights of the photographer or artist.

▲ **Step 2: Prepare to trace the image.** Start with a sheet of white paper. Place a piece of carbon paper over the white paper. Place the image on top of the carbon paper. Secure the stack to the table with masking tape.

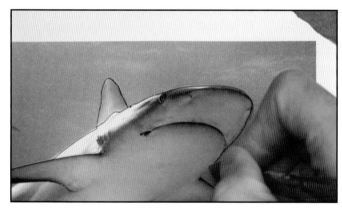

▲ **Step 3: Trace the lines.** Decide how much detail to include; what areas will be shadows or negative space and what areas will be solid wood. Use a colored pen so you can see where you've already traced. Shade or mark an *X* in the areas to be cut out.

▲ **Step 4: Identify any floaters.** All the white areas need to be connected. Areas that are surrounded by shadows or negative space will fall out when cut. Eyes are a particularly troublesome area. Take time to identify where light would shine off the pupil of the eye, and connect that light to the nearest solid area.

▲ **Step 5: Examine the pattern.** Keeping one side of the stack taped in place, peel back the photo and carbon paper and decide if the amount of detail is right for you. Replace the top layers and add more shadows or detail lines if desired.

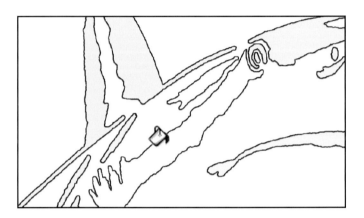

▲ **Step 6: Scan the pattern (optional).** Scanning the pattern into a computer allows you to check for any problem areas and save the pattern for future use. Several programs have a "fill" feature that allow you to shade the sections to be cut. This fill will alert you to any line breaks or floaters that should be corrected before you attempt to cut the pattern. I use Paint Shop Pro software, which lets me clean up the lines and shade the areas to be cut out.

## WOOD AND BLADE SELECTION

Selecting the stock for your finished portrait and the tools you use to cut the pattern is essentially a matter of personal choice. While personal preferences in scrolling can be compared to an individual's choices in automobiles, there are some general guidelines when it comes to portrait-style cutting.

The photo on the left shows the bland grain pattern of birch. The photo on the right shows how several plys are joined together to form Baltic birch plywood.

### Wood Selection

Portrait-style cuttings can be very intricate. In many cases, the bridges between different elements are extremely thin. That is why most people use Baltic birch plywood for these types of projects.

The advantage of Baltic birch plywood is the number of thin layers, or plys, that are glued together to make the wood. The grain rotates 90° between each ply, which adds to the overall strength of the wood. Since most portraits are framed, they are usually cut from ⅛" to ¼"-thick plywood. That way you can fit them into a standard picture frame.

Another advantage to the thin wood is that you can stack cut several portraits at the same time. Using plywood means that you can orient your pattern in any direction without regard to the surface grain. The grain of the interior plys run perpendicular to the grain of the surface ply.

Baltic birch is also known for its bland grain and creamy, white color. This lack of grain character makes it a good choice for portraits, where an intricate grain pattern could distract from the overall image. That is not to say that you can't cut a portrait out of some other kind of wood. It just takes a bit more caution.

To cut a portrait out of solid wood, you need to examine the fragile areas of the pattern and orient the pattern so those areas are not in a short-grain area.

Short grain areas are areas where the grain lines run perpendicular to the wood. The wood is fragile in these areas and prone to breakage.

To cut portraits in hardwood, I suggest stock at least ½"-thick. That makes it more difficult to stack cut, but you can still sandwich the solid wood between a layer or two of plywood. Solid wood pieces should be glued to a wooden backing board when finished for maximum support.

A close up photo illustrates the difference between a spiral blade (top) and a regular blade (bottom).

## Blades

Although I have seen scrollers use regular blades to cut portrait-style projects, I prefer to use spiral blades. A spiral scroll saw blade is twisted so the cutting teeth are present on all sides. Spiral blades let you cut in any direction without rotating the wood. In addition to portrait-style cutting, spiral blades are often used for large pieces, where it would be impractical to rotate the stock on the saw table.

Some scrollers have a difficult time cutting with spiral blades. Traditional scroll saw techniques suggest you back the wood up against the blade to make a sharp turn; if you back up against a spiral blade, it will cut the wood. It can also be difficult to cut a straight line with a spiral blade. If you haven't used a spiral blade before, take some time to practice on a piece of scrap wood before beginning to cut your portrait. If you prefer the control of a regular blade, I suggest a small size to allow you to cut the detail necessary in most portrait work.

For most of my projects, I use a #0 or #2 spiral blade. These blades are fine enough that I can cut the detailed areas, but durable enough that I am not constantly breaking blades.

## CUTTING A PORTRAIT-STYLE PROJECT

Portrait-style projects are cut the same way any other fretwork is cut. It consists of drilling blade-entry holes and inserting the blade through each hole to cut that particular section of negative space. For most portraits, I attach two or more pieces of plywood together to stack cut several projects at once. There are three main methods to stack cut:

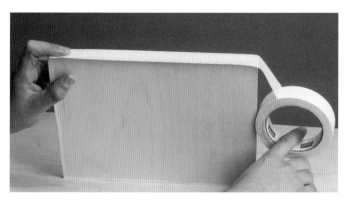

### Tape the edges
Wrap masking tape around the edges. This works well if your wood is totally flat, but it doesn't support the middle area if you are cutting a large, bowed piece.

### Tape Between the Layers
Apply strips of double-sided tape between the layers. Position the tape in large sections of waste area whenever possible and cut those sections last. It takes a bit longer to cut and place the double-sided tape, but if you spread the tape pieces out evenly across the portrait, it will provide better support.

### Brads through waste areas
Drive small nails or brads into several waste areas throughout the portrait. A brad nailer makes this easy, but you can nail the brads in by hand. Cut these waste areas last to maintain the integrity of the stack. Be sure to sand smooth any overhanging nails or brads on the bottom of your stack to avoid damage to your saw table.

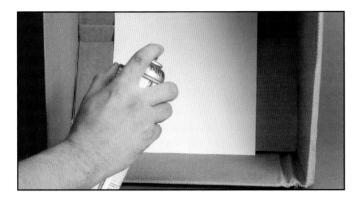

▲ **Step 1: Transfer the pattern to the blank.** Apply spray adhesive to the back of the pattern. Place the pattern inside a cardboard box to control overspray. Apply the pattern to the blank. Smooth out any bubbles. You can add a layer of clear packaging tape on top of the pattern to help lubricate the blade as you cut.

## FINISHING THE PORTRAIT

After spending several hours, or even days, cutting a detailed portrait, you may be tempted to take short cuts in the finishing stage. Careful attention to sanding and finishing will highlight your work; rushing through this portion of the project will be evident in the completed portrait.

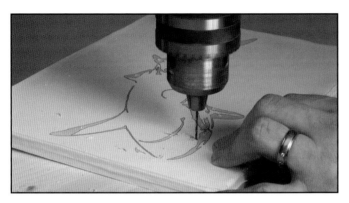

▲ **Step 2: Drill blade-entry holes for each waste area.** I use a $1/16$"-diameter drill bit for as many holes as I can; it is easier to thread the blade through the larger hole. Switch to a #66 drill bit for small areas. Drill the holes perpendicular to the blank.

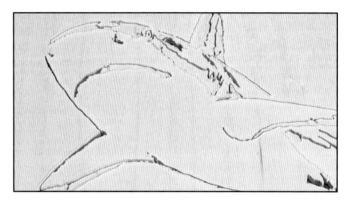

▲ **Step 1: Return the cut-out pieces to the waste areas.** You can hand sand each cut, but it's easier to return the cut outs to the piece and then sand the project as a single sheet. Replacing the waste areas provides added support to fragile areas.

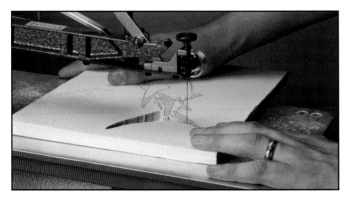

▲ **Step 3: Cut the waste areas.** Make sure the saw table is square to the blade; any deviations from square are compounded when you stack cut. Thread the blade through the blade-entry holes. Carefully cut the design. Keep the cut-out pieces. These will be replaced into the portrait to support fragile areas when you sand.

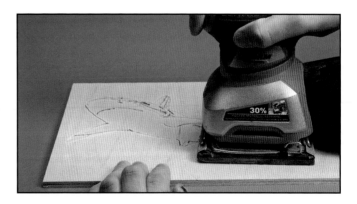

▲ **Step 2: Sand the front and back of the portrait.** I use a palm sander and 220-grit sandpaper. Use caution, because there will be fragile areas. You can also lay the sandpaper on a flat surface and slide the finished project over the sandpaper. I hand sand any delicate areas.

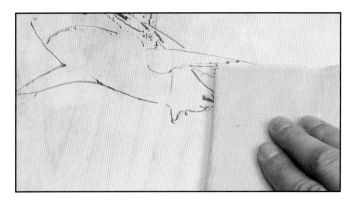

▲ **Step 3: Remove the sanding dust.** Use compressed air or a tack cloth. If you do happen to break a piece when sanding, glue it back in place with cyanoacrylate (CA) glue after all the sanding dust has been removed.

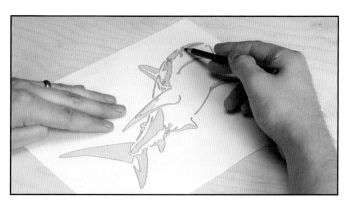

▲ **Step 1: Choose the areas to color.** Take an extra pattern and add a bit of color to different areas. Sometimes less is more when it comes to staining. A subtle hint of color can accent the contrast between the light wood and dark backer board.

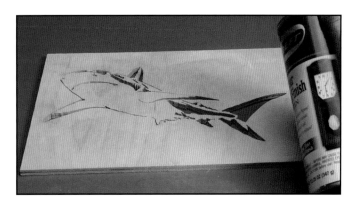

▲ **Step 4: Apply a coat of spray lacquer.** Spray lacquer is a durable finish when the piece is framed, and it disguises any areas you glued back together with CA glue. Apply a light coat, allow it to dry according to the manufacturer's instructions, and sand it lightly with 220-grit sandpaper to remove any high spots. Apply three or four light coats, sanding lightly between each coat.

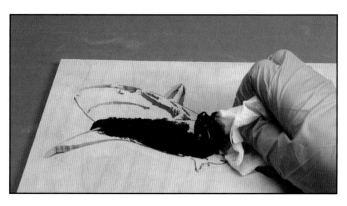

▲ **Step 2: Apply the stain.** Carefully wipe the gel on with the corner of a rag, wait a few minutes, and wipe it off with a clean corner.

## STAINING A PORTRAIT

Staining is an ideal way to add your own creative touch to the project. Gel-based stains are easy to apply with a rag, and the gel texture allows you to apply the stain right where you want it without worrying about it running. If you are going to add stains to your portrait, do so before applying the spray lacquer. You may not even need to add spray lacquer after staining. In some cases, such as when you cut the portrait from a hardwood, it may be beneficial to apply a light coat of lacquer before staining. Experiment on scrap wood first to test the end results before applying stain to your finished cutting.

▲ **Step 3: Blend the stains together (optional).** In some areas, I apply two colors of stain right next to each other. Then after I wipe off most of the stain, I draw my finger down the line between them, pulling a bit of stain from each side into the center. The blending makes the transition between the colors look more natural.

## DISPLAYING A PORTRAIT

Because portrait-style projects depend on the contrast of negative and positive areas, a backer board of a contrasting color is needed. This is another way to add a creative touch to your portrait. Using different colors for sections of the backer board is an ideal way to add interest to the piece. Use the pattern or completed project to pencil in areas to paint different colors. This method will highlight certain elements of your portrait; for example, the backer board for a duck portrait could use blue for the water and black for the duck.

Add a few coats of spray paint to a piece of plywood to create a quick and easy backer board.

Cut a piece of thin plywood to the same dimensions as your finished project and spray paint the board black. The backer board can also be made from cardboard or foam core. Attach the backer board to the portrait with CA glue or epoxy, or use a frame to keep the backer board in place.

If you cut your portrait from Baltic birch, a frame will hide the multiple layers of wood that make up the plywood and lend a polished look to your project. The glass and backer board also help to protect the fragile areas.

The easiest method is to size your portrait to fit a commercial frame. If you size the portrait correctly, it will fit into an 8" x 10" frame. You could put the same portrait into an 11" x 14" frame with matting. Framing is really a personal decision. I have seen portraits framed with beautiful custom frames, and others with inexpensive discount-store frames.

Portraits cut from solid wood can also be framed, although some of the most striking portraits I've seen are cut from slabs of wood with the bark still attached. These pieces, with a simple black backing and hanger attached to the back, really stand out in a crowd.

One of the primary advantages to portrait-style projects is their versatility. With a bit of forethought, you can turn a portrait into a clock, a box lid, a coat rack, or even a set of bookends. You are limited only by your imagination.

Add these wildlife designs to projects such as coat racks, box lids, or cabinet doors.

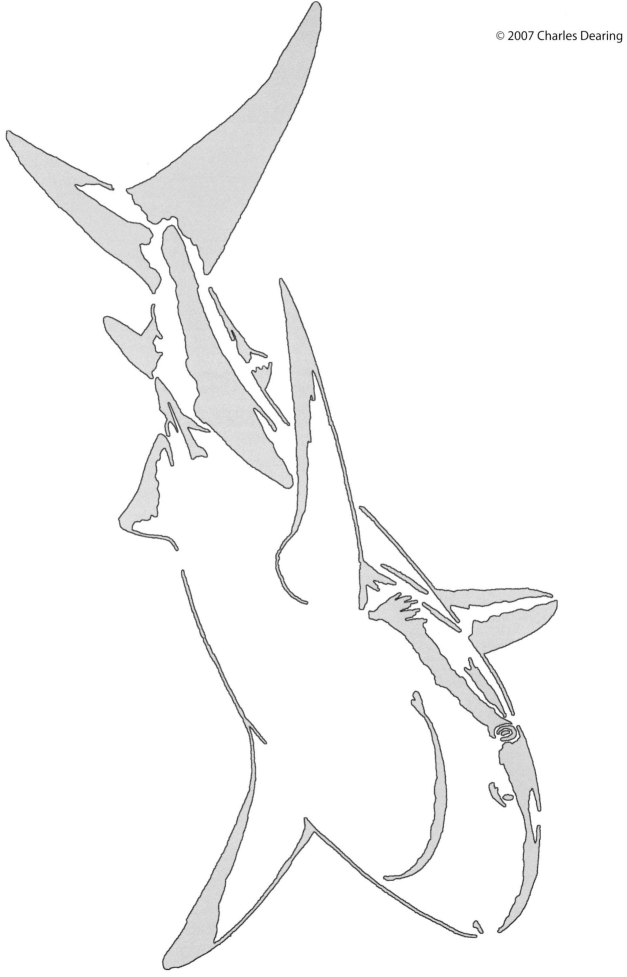

WILDLIFE PORTRAITS IN WOOD

FOX CHAPEL
PUBLISHING

FREE PATTERN OFFER
FOX CHAPEL PUBLISHING CO INC
1970 BROAD ST
EAST PETERSBURG PA 17520-1102

# FREE Pattern OFFER!

## GET Creative with these Fantastic Patterns!

**YES!** Please send me the Free Pattern indicated below

☐ Woodcarving  ☐ Scroll Saw  ☐ Pyrography  ☐ Woodworking  ☐ Woodturning

Name

Address                                    City

State/Prov.                                Zip

Country

Email

**BONUS** Enter your email address to receive more free patterns and special offers!

Return card or complete online for instant access to free patterns:
**www.foxchapelpublishing.com/free-pattern**

*Cut by Neal Moore*

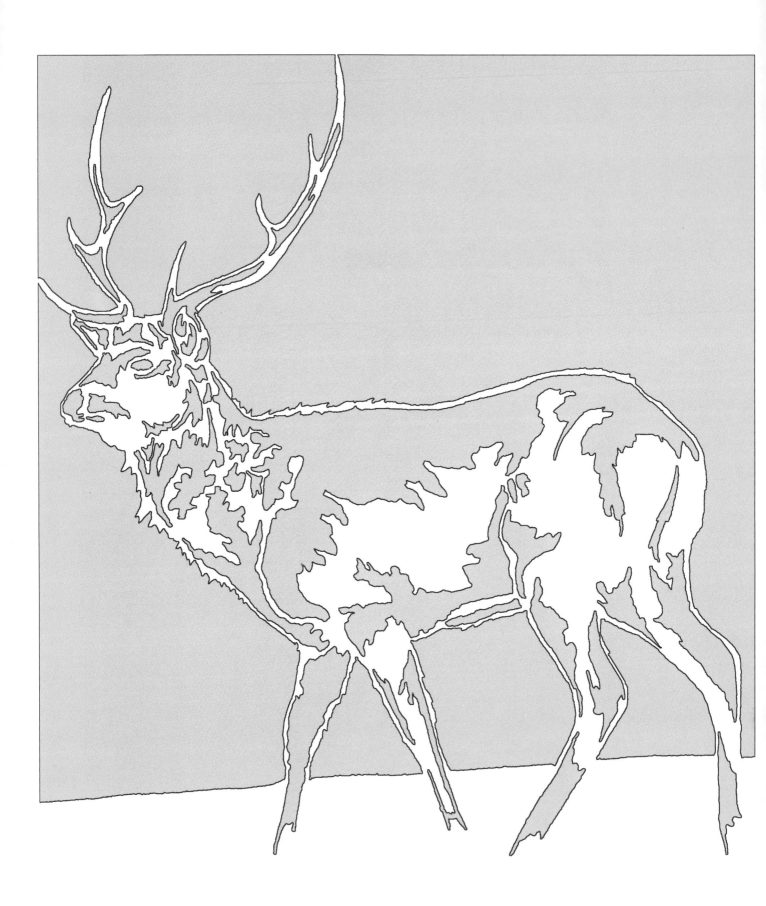

© 2007 Charles Dearing

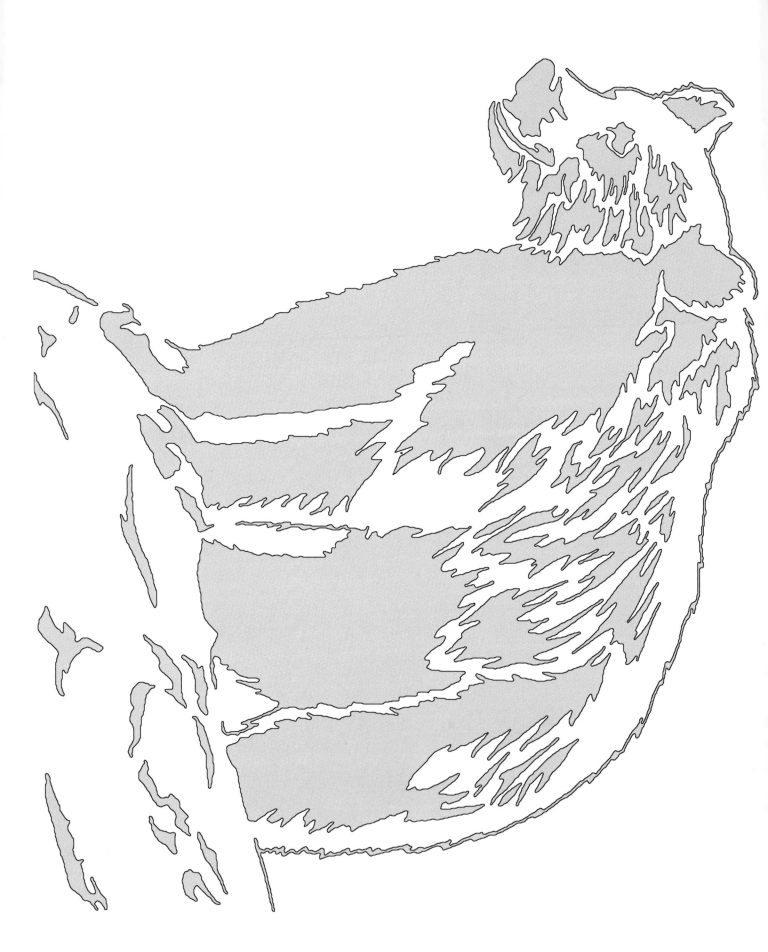

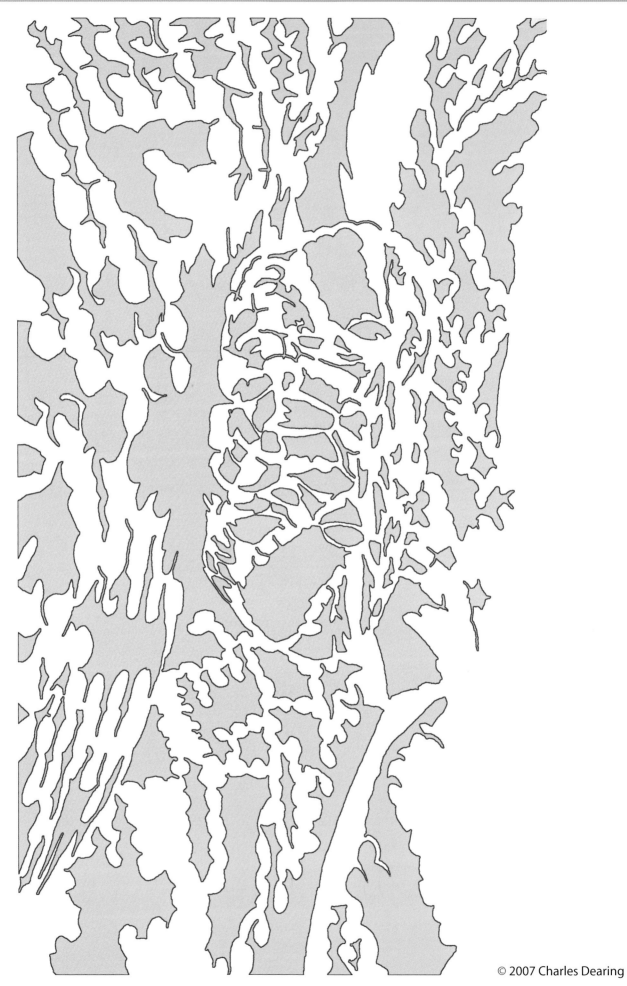

*Cut by Dale Helgerson*

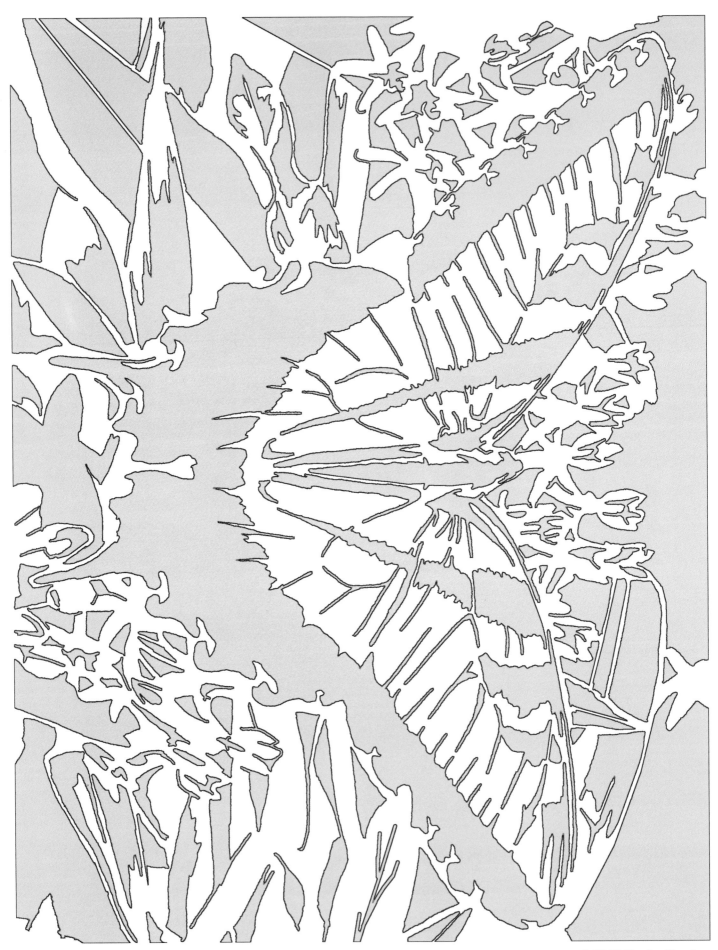

*Cut by Dale Helgerson*

*Cut by Neal Moore*

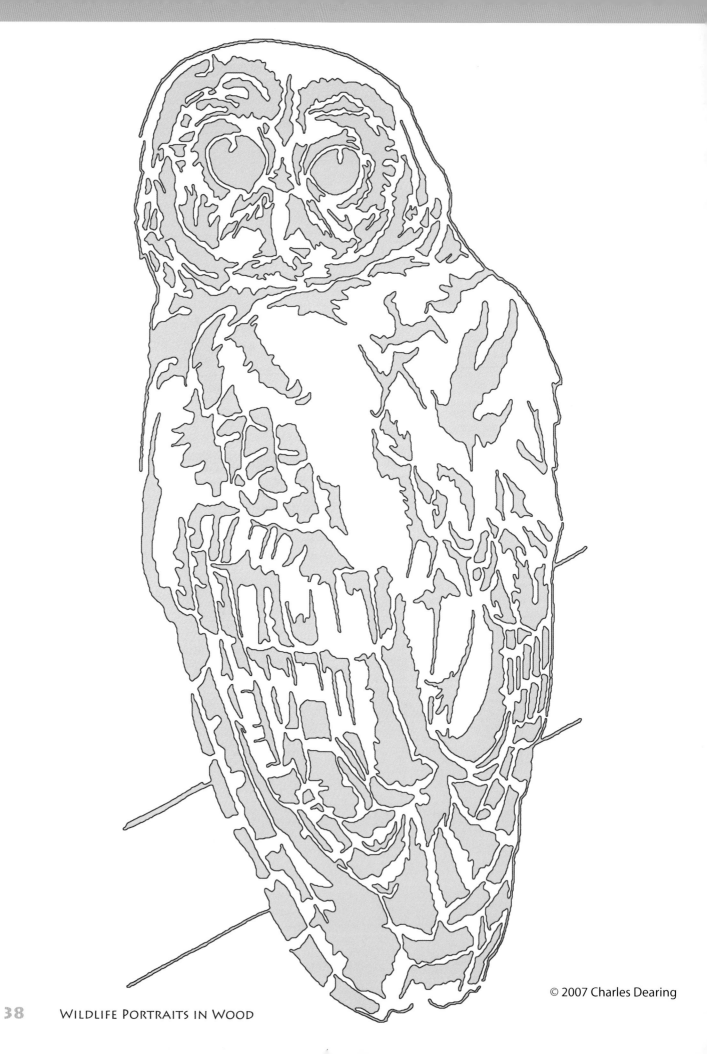

WILDLIFE PORTRAITS IN WOOD

*Cut by Dale Helgerson*

*Cut by Dale Helgerson*

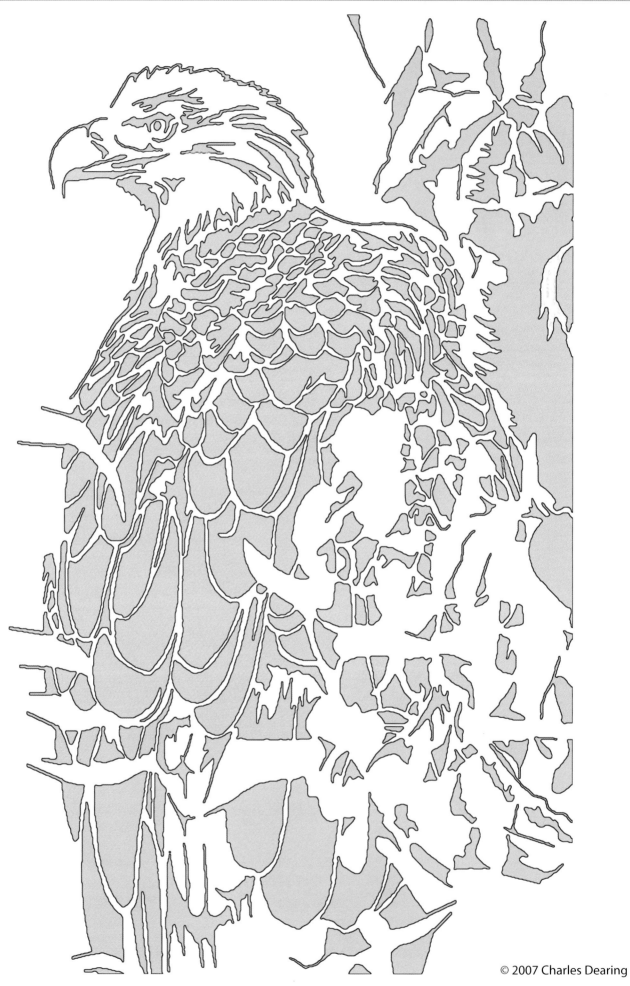

© 2007 Charles Dearing

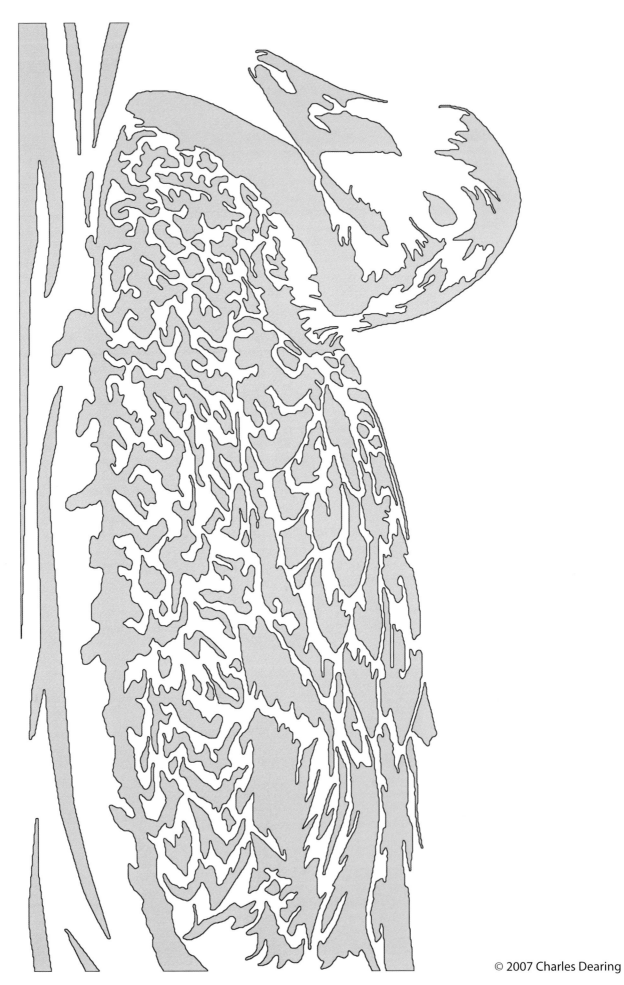

*Cut by Neal Moore*

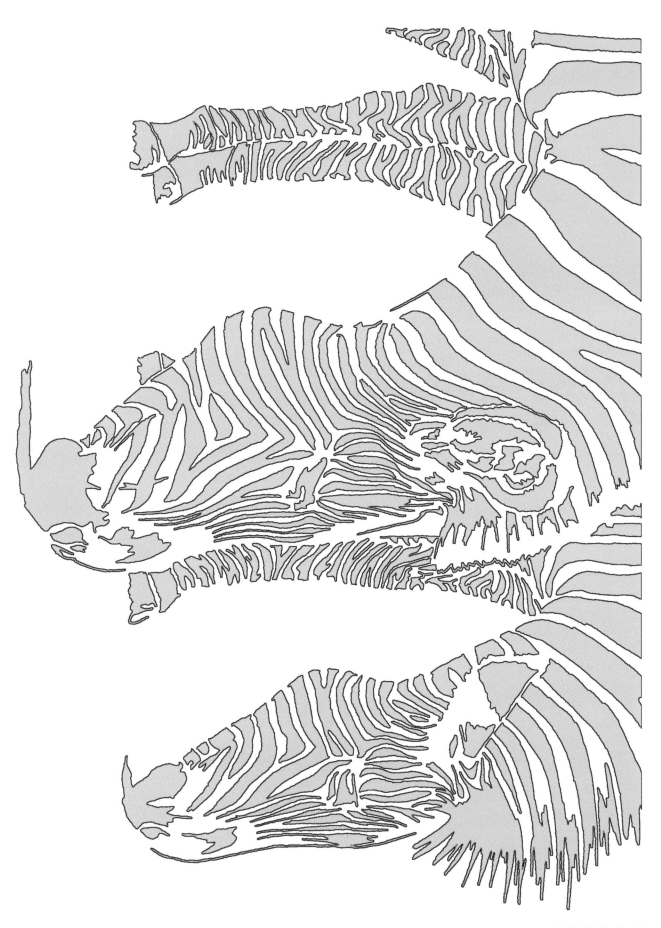

© 2007 Charles Dearing

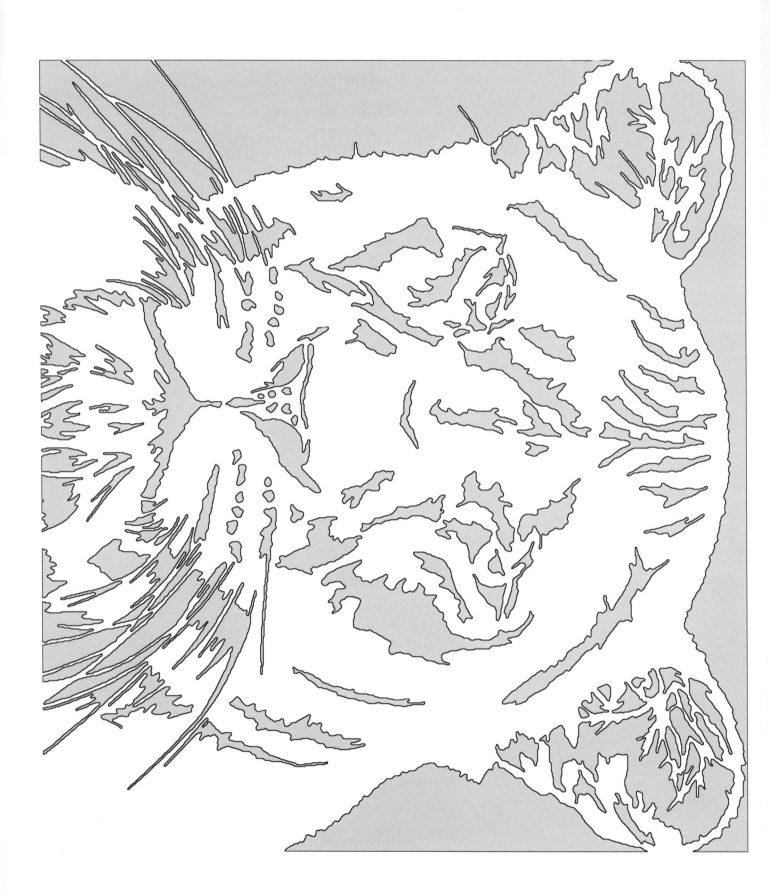

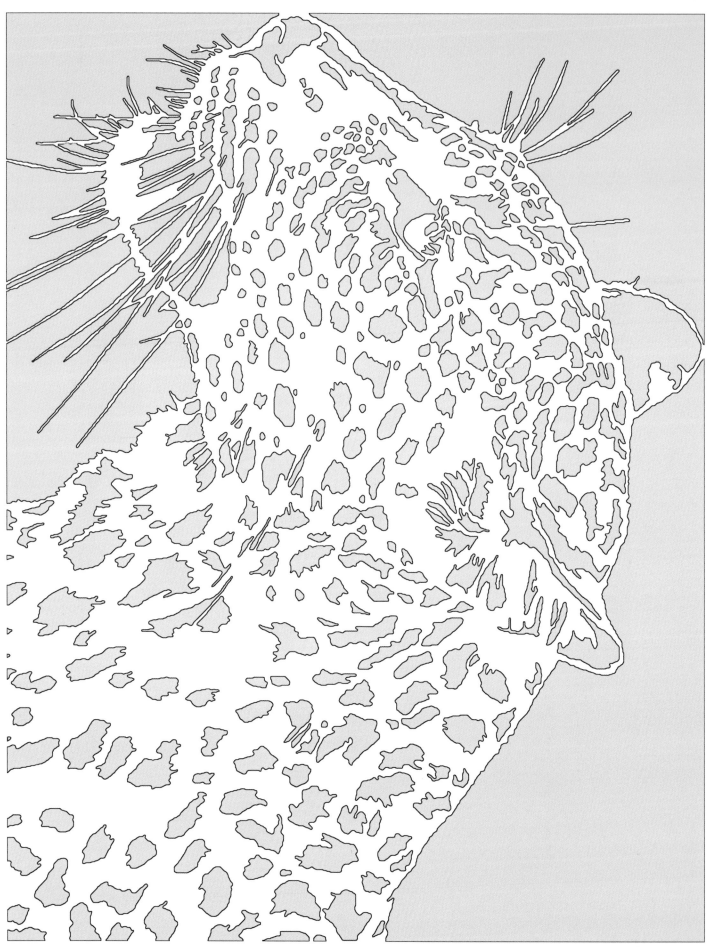

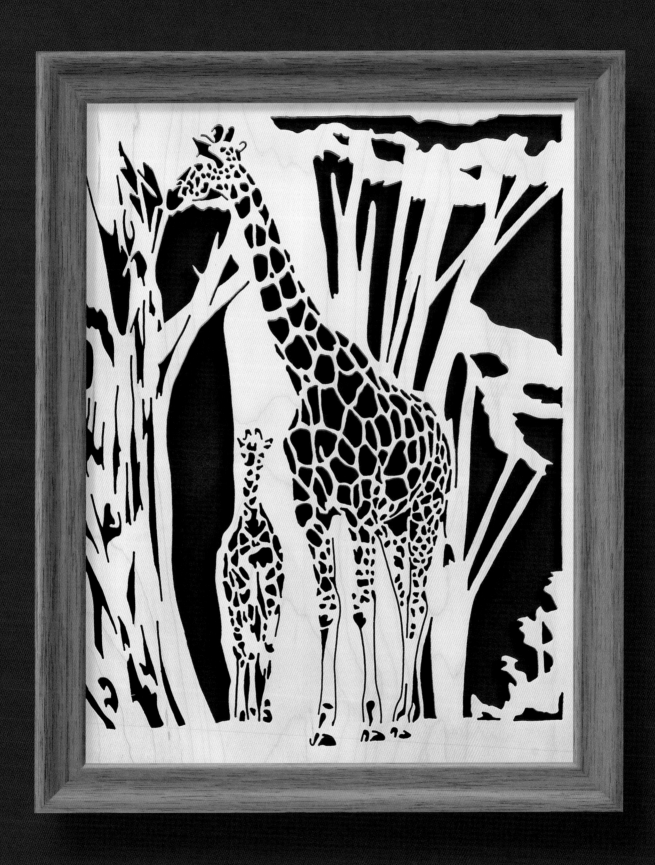

# More Great Books from Fox Chapel Publishing

### Intarsia Woodworking Projects
*By Kathy Wise*
21 original full-size patterns enclosed in a bound-in pouch. Includes step-by-step tutorials for beginners & experts alike.

**$19.95**
ISBN 978-1-56523-339-3

### Animal Puzzles for the Scroll Saw
*By Judy & Dave Peterson*
26 ready-to-cut patterns to create fascinating free-standing puzzles of your furry & feathered friends.

**$14.95**
ISBN 978-1-56523-255-6

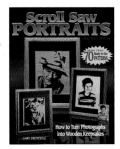

### Scroll Saw Portrait
*By Gary Browning*
Turn a favorite photogra into a scroll sawed masterpiece. Also include patterns for pets, animals famous faces, and more!

**$14.95**
ISBN 978-1-56523-251-8

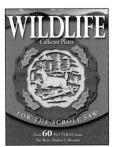

### Wildlife Collector Plates for the Scroll Saw
*By Rick & Karen Longabaugh*
60 wildlife patterns that capture the splendor of nature. Bonus plans for a plate holder included.

**$16.95**
ISBN 978-1-56523-300-3

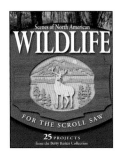

### Scenes of North American Wildlife for the Scroll Saw
*By Rick & Karen Longabaugh*
25 scenic patterns featuring lush landscapes and a wide variety of popular wildlife.

**$16.95**
ISBN 978-1-56523-277-8

### Birds of North America for the Scroll Saw
*By Rick & Karen Longabaugh*
25 projects capture the beauty of the Bald Eagle, Canada Goose, and much more!

**$16.95**
ISBN 978-1-56523-312-6

## LOOK FOR THESE BOOKS AT YOUR LOCAL BOOKSTORE OR WOODWORKING RETAILE

### To order direct, call 800-457-9112 or visit www.FoxChapelPublishing.com

By mail, please send check or money order + $4.00 per book for S&H to:
Fox Chapel Publishing, 1970 Broad Street, East Petersburg, PA 17520

# Learn from the Experts

You already know that Fox Chapel Publishing is a leading source for woodworking books, videos, and DVDs, but did you know that we also publish *Scroll Saw Woodworking & Crafts*? Published quarterly, *Scroll Saw Woodworking & Crafts* is the magazine scroll saw enthusiasts turn to for the premium projects and expert information from today's leading wood crafters. Contact us today for your free trial issue!

# SCROLLSAW
## Woodworking & Crafts

- Written by today's leading scroll saw artists
- Dozens of attractive, shop-tested patterns and project ideas for scrollers of all skill levels
- Great full-color photos of step-by-step projects and completed work-presented in a clear, easy-to-follow format
- Keep up with what's new in the scrolling community with tool reviews, artist profiles, and event coverage

**Subscribe Today!** 888-840-8590 • www.scrollsawer.com